MW01098750

Letters and Sounds

Ee

SCHOOL PUBLISHERS

Photos:
Cover, © Superstock; p. 2, © Harcourt Telescope; p. 3, © Harcourt Index; p. 4, © Harcourt Index; p. 5, © Superstock; p. 6, © Harcourt Index; p. 7, © Superstock; p. 8, © Harcourt Telescope.

Printed in China

ISBN-13: 978-0-15-358378-0
ISBN-10: 0-15-358378-9

Ordering Options
ISBN 10: 0-15-358355-X (Grade K Below-Level Collection)
ISBN 13: 978-0-15-358355-1 (Grade K Below-Level Collection)
ISBN 10: 0-15-360631-2 (package of 5)
ISBN 13: 978-0-15-360631-1 (package of 5)

4 5 6 7 8 9 10 0940 15 14 13 12 11 10 09

e

e

e

e

e

e

e